Z

WITHDRAWN

COLLECTED POEMS

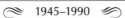 1945–1990

COLLECTED POEMS
≈ 1945–1990 ≈

Barbara Howes

THE UNIVERSITY OF ARKANSAS PRESS
Fayetteville 1995

99   98   97   96   95   5   4   3   2   1

Designed by Gail Carter

☺ The paper used in this publication meets the minimum
requirements of the American National Standard for Perma-
nence of Paper for Printed Library Materials Z39.48-1984.

Library of Congress Cataloging-in-Publication Data
Howes, Barbara.
   The collected poems of Barbara Howes, 1945–1990 /
Barbara Howes.
       p.   cm.
   ISBN 1-55728-335-4 (cloth : alk. paper). — ISBN 1-55728-336-2
(paper : alk. paper)
   I. Title.
PS3515.0924A6   1995
811'.54—dc20   94-32343
                                                        CIP

Certain poems in this collection first appeared in *The Undersea
Farmer* (The Banyan Press, 1948); *In the Cold Country* (Bonacio and
Saul with Grove Press, 1954); *Light and Dark* (Wesleyan University
Press, 1959); *Looking Up at Leaves* (Alfred A. Knopf, 1966); *The Blue
Garden* (Wesleyan University Press, 1972); *A Private Signal: Poems New
and Selected* (Wesleyan University Press, 1977); *Moving* (The Elysian
Press, New York, and Cold Spring Harbor, New York, 1983); and
in the following magazines: *Bennington Review, Chimera, Conjunctions,
Harvard Magazine,* and *Inquiry.*

FOR GREGORY AND EVITA

TOGETHER

Love
Grows out of a clouded sky,
Lands. And becomes . . .
It holds so much to offer,
To accept;—though many lie fallow,
Chomping on self only.—
Love is a bond, a release, a
Private signal. It stays.
It moves . . . Two
As one: As two: For both
It glows all that long green
Enduring voyage . . . (For me,
It is as if each day
They bring me flowers . . .)

FROM *The Undersea Farmer* (1948)

FOR WILLIAM JAY SMITH

FROM *In the Cold Country* (1954)

FOR XIMENA DE ANGULO

FROM *Light and Dark* (1959)

FOR HARRIOT ALLEN

FROM *Looking Up at Leaves* (1966)

FOR CHARLEE AND DICK WILBUR

FROM *The Blue Garden* (1972)

FOR DAVID AND GREGORY

FROM *A Private Signal* (1977)

FOR ELEANOR AND RED WARREN

Translations

Wonders (1983–1990)

FOR PRISCILLA HOWES GRANT

EVERYWOMAN

Oh, where are you riding, lady,
So fast on your mindless horse?
What wonder has set the compass
That leads you this skyline course;
What goal or what comfort, lady,
Call with such force?

Oh, where are you riding, riding?
For autumn burns in the eyes
Of those you pass so gaily
In your fresh greening guise;
The leaves have sickened, lady,
And their sap dries.

Oh, where, oh, where are you riding?
Your horse is a hollow gong
Whose hoofbeats fade to an echo
As thin as your wisp of song;
No flesh to your grasp, none, lady,
And the nights grow long.

THE LOST GIRL

The wise Irish have it that the circle
Dew-marked in the deep sward is where
The little people danced: their fairy ring,
Their empery within this demarcation.
We cut our circles in the ice of rooms
Where by firelight two skaters glide
In friendship, courtship, hatred—for love or doom
Are they bound tighter in their circling
Till life can never be the same for each.
Or as any group, meeting at hazard, skiers,
Or housemaid and butler leveled below stairs,
Soon feel grow round them this retaining wall,
A group's invisible and plastic caul.

The girl from her charmèd circle has strayed away,
Incomprehensibly lost; we were all here,
In her subtraction everything is changed;
The face of the world is askew, fear knocks knocks knocks,
Our round floor tilts, we are queasy with questioning,
Dreading the answer, dreading we may not hear;
Walls crumble, we are shaken and spilled like eggs
In a wreck, all thrown, addled, of a sudden alone.
Days scud away, so by disaster blown.

The land, on a map, runs out secure and clear,
The effortless car disgorges gorged miles,
But space has swollen, an enormity,
Each field is a decade, we falter, cold,
Seeing how many graves the ground can hold.

The circle is broken, splayed in the wide expanse
Of land, too far, too rough, too huge for search;
Has earth cracked open and swallowed her in its spasm?
Sky thunders down upon us, and we fall
Out of God's mouth, down into the reeling chasm.

THE STAG OF GOD

First Congregational Church, Francestown

The neck of the white stag of the valley
Yearns toward the sky with such grace
That his soul can but continue this aspiration
Further in space;

Firm-moulded spire of ivory
Stretched up, up, as if to touch
The tenderest spiced leaves in Eden.
No distrust

Deepens the shadows of his eyes
Or sets the muscles of his sturdy shoulders
Jangling. The cool powerful basilica
Of his body holds

Firm in the agony of spring
And in the passion of the storm,
White and firm after all the years that crept
By his white form.

Yet the bleached stag of the valley
Has no shadow to cast upon the earth
To warm it, no full-throated gospel call
To reach every hearth;

His mighty haunches hold but do not spring
Forward and outward in sympathy
Or penance; were he ever to regain
Sinew and elasticity

He might not, high and cold upon the land
Outworn as the poor Ark on Ararat,
Look useless down while the tormented world
Seeks past that spot.

THE SPORT OF BOYS

Seeing the wild boys on the beach,
The cruel waves strike the shore
From far in a small boat
Where the long draw
Up and fall of waters
Lulled us, slow
Tides beneath and all
At anchor though
In motion. Seeing the waves'
Monotonous thrust
Upward on sand on crabs
Wetting the nests
Of leathery weathered weeds,
A great sower
Casting its watery seed
Upon the shore
In slow dispassionate rhythm
Only ceasing
When tides turn over.
Exultant ring
Of childish voices calls
Our eyes. They run
Up and down, with stout
Sticks flailing one
Slow crustacean after
Another, crushing—
Jackdaws beaked for havoc—
Destroying hurting
In ecstasy of pointless
Cruelty. God
Knows men love to kill:
Jesse's rod
Has turned into a club,
And we, far off,
Shocked, so far, our shout
Faint as a cough.

THE NEW LEDA

Goosegirl, your feet are slow
And heavy with acceptance, while the echo
Of what will come
Gathers momentum and batters at your eardrum.

The future hangs
Over you like an airborne bell, its clangs
Will gut your heart, will keep
Up their reverberant assault, no sleep

Will be the same again;
Marked, muted by this inexorable hyphen
You cannot be the same;
There is no sanctuary, the god will come

And bed you in his plumage;
Intent, bird-lidded, knotted in his rage
Of lust he will flail down
Every abject appeal. . . . Quiet in gown

Of white the bride of Christ
Moves down the waiting nave as if her wrist
Were held and she led,
Hands heart obeying the seeing unseen Dead,

And she led on as though
Walking through shallow water, where the slow
Tide urges at her feet
But checks their driftwood longing. Will the sweet,

Wan, dedicated face,
Inward as some old painting, find a place
Of sweetest rest, a home
Now in the Spirit's mansion and catacomb?

Will she encounter love,
Laughter, pain, and grief, or will she live

For centuries encased
In waterglass serenity, the taste

Of an eternal death
In life upon her lips, although breath
Cannot fail? Her
Limbo holds her like a fly in amber,

Beyond the reach of life.
Sisters, wastrels, when will you have enough
Of sacrifice and harm
And deprivation? Remember the mighty arm

That, white and sick with strain,
Wrestled the whole night out until the plain
Was light and he could see,
Deep down the precipice of self, his adversary

And ask his blessing. Either
Make peace with yourselves, or live locked in such war
As, ruinous from the start,
Turns dark with pity Jacob's brazen heart.

THE BAR AT THE CAROUSEL

Cloche-hatted like Hermes, game-feathered for wings,
Emotion drives her body as one leans
Against the storm-swept tiller, features sharp
With rage and sting.

She sits there, perches, while her love, her friend,
Placed doll-like between her and the man
Revolves in coquetry, the prey of each,
Who both intend

That she shall wear their colors, turning now
To the distraught rouged mask, then to the man's
Jowled face, his eyes like pegs, but free in the world
To come or go.

The rioting heart of Sappho's stormy daughter
Sends out hate which even he can feel
Who takes his leave abruptly, caring little;
The usual slur

Of the world falls off like spray from a plunging bow.
She aches with triumph, and the muscles round
Her thin lips swell with power, a pretty death-
Mask quickening now.

In this museum, the world, we have a fine
Prospect of ancient gods, nor should we fail
To recognize here Hermes as death's agent.
The androgyne

At home in her half-world, woman's companion,
Seneschal among the shadows, waits
To guide her curving way until she wanders
All compass gone.

LADY-POET

The Lady-Poet's experience unravels doom.
Her cool and sickly fingers beat tattoos
On wicker furniture, the while her soul
Erupts the volumes of its phantasies.

Unwarmed by man, her heart is swathed unseen
By latticed terraces, and by the green
Tincture-of-silk seductions she has sown.

In rarefied and astigmatic tone
She flings the tally of her injuries,
Made whole and potent, at the peeping world.

FULL FATHOM FIVE

The day the poem rose up
He was out fishing,
Fathoms above the reef;
The fish curvetted
And the words diverged.

Once when love caromed in his brain,
The squid below spit ciphers at the sun;
His balloon heart swelled, but not one
Line could he get from it.

Out of the grab bag of the mind
One hour's version of the poem is drawn
Framed and fixed.
Use it. Do not look where,
Under the pale survivor, swing
Shades of fairer forms,
Or you will never forget
Their mocking.

THE CRITIC

Ugolino takes his rest,
For rest he needs after such labor;
He has prepared a tasty stew
Neglecting neither sauce nor savor;
His spiritual fathers he has cooked,
Basted, spitted, and sprigged with bay;
His cultural fathers he has eaten,
And now he's quite as great as they.
Great with father sitteth he
Happy, for they are no more:
Eliot, with thyme bedight,
Tossed like Leander to the shore;
Yeats tumbled to oblivion
Without a mourner. Ugolino
Surveys his future dancing bright
As Theda Bara at the Kino.
He wears contentment like a wreath
And for a smile an orange rind;
There is no art but in his belch
Whose stomach's bigger than his mind.

INDIAN SUMMER

This man, this stranger in my arms
Lies quiet now, below in sleep,
Lost in the deep seine of his dream.
How wide the net is cast, far out, far down,
But his dream plumbs himself; mine is my own.

Two feral figures in the jungle half-
Light taut in struggle
Shoulder to shoulder,
Cold hate, colder force
In the leashed clash of wrestlers
Clasped in war in
One another's arms;
There they enact
The ancient drama of possession.
But who has won?
Deep down within the womb
Of dream, of his own dream,
Each acts his part, and is by it possessed.

Time's horn of plenty spills
Out to us her dialectic
Changing forms;
There is no gauging when
Love will take root,
Run wildfire up the heart's trellis. We learn
That we can harbor such diversity,
And firm at last see
The future in our arms,
A golden cataract that comes
Out of our cornucopia of dream.

THE UNDERSEA FARMER

To dream of islands. . . .
The mind's eye moves and planes
Up the incline of sea,
They lie atilt there
Against the horizon. Islands

Are moored on shoals
And tower above the vaults
Of black water, pyramids
Of depth, where old
Benumbed seas chill the shoals;

What arteries
Of light shaft down these fathoms
At length snuff out in black,
The sea-pit water
Muffles even the arteries

Of the imagination
But as it muffles, fills.
Our tines touch depth and surface
As we roll
In our imagination,

In the sea,
In the glaucous sunny deep water
Between worlds. A shark
That goes his easy
Narrative through our sea

Poses a model
Gesture in his here-
To-there progress, long
Curving pentameter
Of skaters; or note a model

Of the oblique in the flying
Fish's brushing shadow
While he high-tails it over
The waves; he grazes
Us only with his dark flying-

Away symbol
For our notebooks and hope and joy;
If we prefer the conceptual
Sea horse, he rides
The waves as if a symbol

Of inwardness mounted
There, flesh tucked beneath
His bony plates, all outline,
But motored
From within; my mounting

Wonder at such
Proliferation allows
But a glance at the shagreen
Sea urchin, delicate
As Christmas-tree ornaments, such

Mystery in
Its being, one can only
Believe that it does breathe.
These denizens
Of form are catalysts in

Our minds; so let us go
Hand over hand back toward
The watery skylight, toward land,
Afraid only of letting
Our subaqueous lifeline go.

VIEWS OF THE OXFORD COLLEGES

Oxford abounds in fern and birdwatcher.
It is a lovely place when its short spring
Softens the chilblained air, and coats the stone
Tombs of buildings with its early green.
It is most lovely to the mind's eye
When age and earnestness discreetly sing.

Prudence and earnestness discreetly sing
Their muted canticles; the eighty-odd-
Year-old, the old at twenty-five, or the
Intelligent wrapped in long mufflers nod
At beauty passing, but their baths are cold,
They have an ague and believe in God.

The ague holds, and the belief in God
Carries them through the valley of depression,
Bleak as any mine, like Cromwell who,
Roundheaded in his obstinacy, rang down
A curtain on felicity; the past
Is moored in Oxford firm as an obsession.

Moored in Oxford firm as an obsession,
Man opens his umbrella which will turn
Back the sensual sun; he cannot feel—
Poor dampened Adam—love or beauty burn
Caught within the spokes of that black wheel.
Oxford abounds in birdwatcher and fern.

BEACON HILL

*. . . for I am a jealous God, visiting the iniquity of the fathers
upon the children unto the third and fourth generation . . .*

Solemnity is a good thing, as far as that goes,
But soon an anaconda ring around
The throat grows out of it, and every gust
Of laughter and huzza is cut off short.

What fear in the hearts of my ancestors so froze
Their throats that not a breath of passion wound
Through them? What flinty habit of distrust
Fired their prayers with all Hell's colors, caught

Life everywhere red-handed? By degree
Their sensibility shrank to a reserve
Deep as their forests, or ran out in trade—
Night prowlers crouched by streams, gaunt glutted mills.

The throat soon learns to take the collar, to be
Thin and cold, the neck soon learns to curve
Forward in starched obedience, the decayed
Veins throbbing under the tightening ring, until

Love and imagination that are thrust
Below, jet forth their darkening phantasies
That hood the mind and impregnate its deep
Fissures with the vivid seeds of waste;

Excess and madness thrive where decorum lusts
After itself and lightly guarantees
Indifference—or else the quick passions leap,
Flood, hurtle, till they choke the throat to rest.

But still the burden of this heritage
Subdues the voice that would cry out in rage.

NO HIDING PLACE DOWN THERE

The South softened and wooed me,
I soon lost
The fettered Northern glance
And covert search for warmth,
Letting time ramble past.

Musing,
I see the days
Float in the sun-drenched air,
Whose sly timelessness devours them
As sun the unmarked dew.
Tranquilly I look where
The land runs out on all sides to the sky,
Delights in its horizons,
A splendid and exhaustless tide;
And, deep, bears easily its warm expanse,
Carries the full intent of nature—
Such tropic possibility,
Such lazy, latent, sure-blooming growth-sympathy
From cotton's honest bolls to green
Frieze of wisteria on old walls.

Beyond,
Hills sown with timber till they meet the sky,
And cypresses' black grandeur; there
The blurring smoke of night will rise
Pierced only by a bird's untimely call.

Yet have I known the South?
A scene
Night and forgetfulness cannot dispel
Is less kind
And gloves my mind with fear and foreboding:
No haze curtains the road

Where death with such insistence strews
Violence among stray and homeless beasts.
Terrible emblem of some rot within,
Printed a thousandfold,
The South wears
This casual knotted mass of blood and fur,
Known only to the carrion rain and sun.

CARPE DIEM

In appreciation of Gertrude Bell (1868–1926)

Some morning I will be old;
What can I say of myself then?

Mind has mattered so much, and knowledge
Is bottomless as the golden bowl
In the myth, ceaseless as light, grave,
Unemptiable as the sea. One's whole

Being pleads for it, and each
Draught gives ladders to the mind;
One looms and cuts new notches on
The door. And yet what discipline

It takes! The ducks in the shooting-gallery
World roll round too quick again
For more than recognition, never
Grasped whole by the prehensile brain.

For all phenomena we have
So little time, and for perfection
Less. To know, to understand
Has been my passion and addiction.

Some morning I will be old;
What can I say of myself then?

To drink so deeply and to have
So much to give, and at the end
To have nothing. This can happen
Easily; as on a journey, we spend

No thought on where we are; the rumored
Hills are like gold to pioneers,
Monopolizing sight; we travel
Too far beyond ourselves to seize

Anything from the day. And now
Longing has settled in my lips
And there is no man I can tell
Of it; no knowledge has equipped

Or cautioned me to hold the day
Firmly in mind and hands; each blue
Resinous hour disappears
Like smoke, forgotten and obscure.

Some morning I will be old;
What can I say of myself then?

That having found no substitute
For love, and of its golden bowl
Wrought no replica within, I live
Alone in the gathering darkness of my soul.

PRIMAVERA

The horse with consumption coughed like the end of the world.
We heard its tremblors echo in that dry bark,
But on our carriage rolled; we minted miles,
Like hoops our coined wheels rolled until the dark
Came down upon the city, and gray shade
Merged all the cathedral's zebra stripes; the park
Recessed for night, vendors' flags, bird wings furled.

Onward and on we rode until the dawn.
From jeweled opera box and catacomb
We summoned up the past: released, the ghosts
Came forth in cloth of gold and tilting heaume
In every city street and hornèd lane
Whose flowers pell-mell hung down, geranium foam
From walls all staunch with red, red staunched by stone.

And on and on; where would the journey end?
Giotto conceived a tower in pure air,
Heraldic rainbow, balanced on her shell
All beauty woke in Aphrodite fair
As history's fairest. Now to trespassers
On the volcano's flank the tocsins blare:
Our mare's obsidian hooves foreknelled the end.

PORTRAIT OF AN ARTIST

For dear life some do
Many a hard thing,
Train the meticulous mind
Upon meaning, seek
And find, and yet discard
All that is not of reality's tough rind.

A cool divining rod,
The heart, another tool,
Keen as a hawk's eye,
Supple as water, bends
Responsive to all four
Humors. In many sympathy runs dry

Or blots and blurs. To be
Ascetic for life's sake,
Honest and passionate,
Is rare. I think of those
Images of Buddha placed
In shells, and later found encased in pearl.

IN A PROSPECT OF FLOWERS

Of a painter drowned
in his twentieth year

As in his tomb
In amethystine water the artist lies,
Framed by raw cement, lapped
By many-petaled sunlight
That engraves
Each phosphorent particle.

He
Hangs there face down,
His body ominous in this design,
Dark head resting on the lapis-lazuli
Empty bosom of water,
Flung
Like Icarus.
Now no vision can again
Furnish those hands with vision
Or
That heart with color.

Royal palms,
The columns of some ancient portico,
Incline;
And we, downcast
At this imagined brink,
Lament and praise—
Within a fatal aquarelle—
The lineaments of the ideal.

COQ DE COMBAT

There Jack-cock struts
Rattling his brassy plumage,
Gamey torso rearing,
Aims his beak
And then,
Oh-ho, lets loose a challenge
That, like darts,
Will smite the target ear,—
Coco-rico!

How can this cocky mobster know
That soon the tumbrils of the night
Will move to harvest darkness,
Or the stars
Like crocuses will close;
The Cyclops moon
All day must be put out,
Its eye interred
In a great vault blue as forget-me-not?

Our brave cock struts:
This very day
May be his day for battle
When, armed cap-à-pie,
All rapier beak and spurs,
Angry, leaping, he'll try
To blood-let and life-let his enemy.
Coco-rico!

Now he,
A feathered timepiece,
Monitor of dawn,
At this gargantuan ring presides,
In his turn bells us out
To do, endure, or die,—
Coco-rico!

MIRROR IMAGE: PORT-AU-PRINCE

Au petit
Salon de Coiffeur,
Monique's ¦ hands fork
like lightning, like a baton
rise ¦ to lead her client's hair
in *repassage:* she irons out the kinks.
Madame's brown cheek ¦ is dusted over with a
paler shade ¦ of costly powder. Nails and lips are red.

Her matching lips and nails incarnadined, ¦ in the
next booth Madam consults her face ¦ imprisoned
in the glass. Her lovely tan ¦ is almost
gone. Oh, watch Yvonne's astute
conductor fingers set the
permanent, ¦ *In little*
Drawing room of
Hairdresser!

RELATIVES

Their eyes go out on stalks like crabs' to the closet;
Sipping their tea they uncoil a précis,
Rumors of shame, malfeasance, bizarre ills
Among the invisible family choir. They covet
Each out-turned glance, all hawsers loaned to land
As I move slowly waterward; they shock
And simper, crouching ringed upon the deck
Rattling the bony dice of tribal fate.
It is time, you jackanapes crew! The moon lets down
The shelled gold of her wake on the river ahead.
It is time to unpilot you; we shall not be late.

THE NUNS ASSIST AT CHILDBIRTH

Robed in dungeon black, in mourning
For themselves they pass, repace
The dark linoleum corridors
Of humid wards, sure in the grace

Of self-denial. Blown by duty,
Jet sails borne by a high wind,
Only the face and hands creep through
The shapeless clothing, to remind

One that a woman lives within
The wrappings of this strange cocoon.
Her hands reach from these veils of death
To harvest a child from the raw womb.

The metal scales of paradox
Tip here then there. What can the nun
Think of the butchery of birth,
Mastery of the flesh, this one

Vigorous mystery? Rude life
From the volcano rolls and pours,
Tragic, regenerate, wild. Sad,
The unborn wait behind closed doors.

DEATH ON THE PLATFORM

As the train moves,
The old man falls
To the hungry wheels.
There is none to aid,
To stop the machine
In its mineral round,
And the frozen earth
Is a cruel confederate.

A child will brave
A nonsensical
But painful spill
From his canting sled,
And on coming clean
Through, will not wonder
About his birth
Or auspice; but, elate,

Climb back, high above
His last perch: taller.
Yet such furies fill
Man's graying head
He must try to sign
Each leaf, confound
Doom with his breath,
To die, at the last, intestate.

The college grove
Where the Chancellor
Kept life at his heels,
Where all men made
Obeisance then
To the scarlet gown,
The rich red heart
Of their intellectual state,

Will lose his love.
He is stricken, all
Is so quickly still.
And the princedom held
With mind, with dream,
Panoply, power
Flees him at death
Who naked speaks of man's blind fate.

MORNING GLORY

For C. W.

Now when spiraling summer burns
Its way toward autumn, on this vine
The morning glory opens such
Buoyant parasols of blue,
Uplifted into light, as to
Recover spring . . . recovering much
More: the azure of a mind
And cloudless heart to which we turn.

IN THE COLD COUNTRY

We came so trustingly, for love, but these
Lowlands, flatlands, near beneath the sea
Point with their cautionary bones of sand
To exorcize, submerge us; we stay free
Only as mermaids glittering in the waves:
Mermaids of the imagination, young
A spring ago, who know our loveliness
Banished, like fireflies at winter's breath,
Because none saw; these vines about our necks
We placed in welcome once, but now as wreath
Against the scalpel cold; still cold creeps in
To grow like ivy over our chilling bodies
Into our blood. Now in our diamond dress
We wive only the sequins of the sea.
The lowlands have rejected us. They lie
Athwart the whispering waters like a scar
On a mirage of glass; the dooming land,
Where nothing can take root but frost, has won.
And what of warmth and what of joy? They are
Sequestered elsewhere, southward, where the sun
Speaks. For all our mermaid vigilance
And balance, all goes under; underneath
The land's gray wave we falter and fall back
To hibernate within the caves of death.

THE DON

A cockney rounds the corner, laundry pins
Upon his nose; a deathshead spouting Greek
Totters abaft the podium: dates of birth
And death sicken the air like blackboard chalk.
The words are mouthed and mumbled till they fall,
Shredded, behind his hand, in the long hall.
This is the scholiast's black mass; we sit
And fret to see each poem impaled, dead
As butterfly on pin, as dried eggshell.
Necromancer of learning, a black bat
With wing extended over literature,
He sweeps to rend Adonis' living body.
Beauty is extinguished, value gone;
Silence in the hall; dark in the hall; all's done.

THE BALCONY

Light playing on the water plays on the trees,
Shimmers and scatters, dowering them with light.
All things partake of the sun's strength,
The long warm hand of heaven is on us until night.

As from a prow that juts in space we watch
Stipple of wind upon the quiet lake,
Each idle insect droning on,
And high above our heads see heron in echelon

Ferry across on deep unhurried wing.
All these foreshortened forms your eyes compose
And render to my understanding,
So that the sunlight too reflects your influence.

Such wisdom near me, I am nearer the light
Whose every incident you so endow.
This is immediacy, this is love;
And by its gracious hand I wake from darkest night.

ANNUNCIATION

Time, a recording angel, bends
One knee upon the grass:
There in the azure close of day
Remote against the arras
Of herb and floweret he broods
On what may come to pass.

Shadows of afternoon arrange
A cloak about her head;
Silent she stands beneath the groined
Portal, awaiting word
Or sign from that ghostly visitor
Of what will be her meed:

Will he say nothing, and she turn
Her back and go within?
Or, waxing, in a little while
Step out upon a scene
Of Tuscan summer, bearing proud
Contour of mandolin?

ON A BOUGAINVILLAEA VINE
AT THE SUMMER PALACE

Under the sovereign crests of dead volcanoes,
See how the lizards move in courtly play;
How when the regnant male
Fills the loose bagpipe of his throat with air,
His mate will scale
Some vine portcullis, quiver, halt, then peer—
Eyes sharp as pins—
At that grandee posed stiff with self-esteem,
His twiglike tail acurve.

What palaces lie hid in vines! She sees
Chameleon greenrooms opening on such
Elite boudoirs,
Flowers as bright as massacres; should she
Not try their spiring tendrils
That like string
Hammocks are slung upon the open air?
Tensing his tiny jaw, he seems to smile;
And while all nature sways,
Lightly rides his delicate trapeze.

A virid arrow parts
The leaves—she's at
His side. Then darts away; he following,
They lose themselves within the redolent shade. . . .
Quiet the palace lies
Under the sun's green thumb,
As if marauding winter would never come.

THE HOMECOMING

All the great voyagers return
Homeward as on an arc of thought;
Home like a ruby beacon burns
As they crest wind, scale wave, soar air;
All the great voyagers return,

Though we who wait never have done
Fearing the piteous accidents,
The coral reef sharp as the bones
It has betrayed, fate's cormorant
Unleashed, whose diving's never done.

Even the voyager of mind
May fail beneath behemoth's weight;
Oh, the world's bawdy carcass blinds
All but the boldest, rots the sails
And swamps the voyaging of the mind.

But all the great voyagers return
Home like the hunter, like the hare
To its burrow; below, earth's axle turns
To speed their coming, the following fair
Winds bless their voyage, blow their safe return.

CHIMERA

After a fearful maze where doubt
Crept at my side down the terrible lightless channel,
I came in my dream to a sandspit parting
Wind-tossed fields of ocean. There,
Lightstepping, appeared
A trio of moose or mules,
Ugly as peat,
Their trotters slim as a queen's.
"Hippocampi!" cried a voice as they sped
Over black water, their salty course,
And away. From the heaving sea
Then sprang a fabulous beast
For its evening gallop.
Head of a lion, goat's head rearing
Back, derisive, wild—the dragon
Body scaling the waves; each reckless
Nature in balance, flying apart
In one. How it sported
Across the water, how it ramped and ran!
My heart took heart. Awaking, I thought:
What was disclosed in this vision
Was good; phantom or real,
I have looked on a noble animal.

EARLY SUPPER

Laughter of children brings
        The kitchen down with laughter.
While the old kettle sings
Laughter of children brings
To a boil all savory things.
        Higher than beam or rafter,
Laughter of children brings
        The kitchen down with laughter.

So ends an autumn day,
        Light ripples on the ceiling,
Dishes are stacked away;
So ends an autumn day,
The children jog and sway
        In comic dances wheeling.
So ends an autumn day,
        Light ripples on the ceiling.

They trail upstairs to bed,
        And night is a dark tower.
The kettle calls: instead
They trail upstairs to bed,
Leaving warmth, the coppery-red
        Mood of their carnival hour.
They trail upstairs to bed,
        And night is a dark tower.

TO W. H. AUDEN ON HIS FIFTIETH BIRTHDAY

Books collide—
Or books in a library do:
Marlowe by Charlotte Mew,
Sir Horace Walpole by Hugh;
The most unlikely writers stand shoulder to shoulder;
One studies incongruity as one grows older.

Symbols collide—
Signs of the zodiac
Range the celestial track,
Pisces has now swung back
Into the lead: we learn to recognize
Each fleck for what it is in our mackerel skies.

Ideas collide—
As words in a poem can.
The poet, Promethean,
Strikes fire in a single line,
Form glows in the far reaches of his brain;
Poets who travel will come home again.

Feeling collides—
Lying for years in wait,
May grope or hesitate.
Now let us celebrate
Feeling, ideas, symbols, books which can
Meet with greatness here within one man.

DANAË

Golden, within this golden hive
Wild bees drone,
As if at any moment they may
Swarm and be gone
From the arched fibers of their cage,
Lithe as whalebone.

Over a pasture, once, I saw
A flock of small
Martins flying in concert, high
Then wheeling, fall;
Like buckshot pent in a string bag
They dotted all

That sky-patch, holding form in their flight,
A vase poured,
Their breathing shape hung in the air—
Below, the road
Fled secretly as quicksilver:
My eyes blurred.

All things come to their pinnacle
Though landscapes shift,
Women sit in the balance, as
Upon a knife;
Irony cuts to the quick—is this
Life or new life?

They sit their years out on a scale,
The heavy yoke
Of their heavy stomachs grounding them—
Or else come back
To barrenness with each full moon;
Minds go slack

Longing, or dreading, that a new
Form will take shape.

(The martins' swarming is a brush stroke
On the landscape,
Within their white-gold, fleshly hall
The wild bees wake.)

Homing at close of day, they meet
This moment: now:
Love calls from its subterranean passage,
The bed they know
May support agony or joy—
To bed they go.

MIDWINTER FLIGHT

Enclosed within its journey, the plane
Lies like the hull of a ship balanced
On ways of air, a war canoe
Jutting into the dark,
A radiant toy
Loosed upon space.
                    Here in this great cocoon
We passengers are pharaohs walled up
With honey, ambergris, grain, and silver
To solace our hibernation.
Or we may be
Glazed ceramic fruit, a still life
Kept for some later century
Under glass.
                  Now while the plane
Tunnels the black massif, we think of other
Things: a circular stair,
Drums, a crimson maple, rainfall, hills,
And checkered moths
Trembling on a lighted pane.

LIGHT AND DARK

Lady, take care; for in the diamond eyes
Of old old men is figured your undoing;
Love is turned in behind the wrinkled lids
To nurse their fear and scorn at their near going.
Flesh hangs like the curtains in a house
Long unused, damp as cellars without wine;
They are the future of us all, when we
Will be dried-leaf-thin, the sour whine
Of a siren's diminuendo. They have no past
But egg husks shattered to a rubbish heap
By memory's looting. Do not follow them
To their camp pitched in a cranny, do not keep
To the road for them, a weary weary yard
Will bring you in; that beckoning host ahead,
Inn-keeper Death, has but to lift his hat
To topple the oldster in the dust. Read,
Poor old man, the sensual moral; sleep
Narrow in your bed, wear no
More so bright a rose in your lapel;
The spell of the world is loosed, it is time to go.

CAT ON COUCH

My cat, washing her tail's tip, is a whorl
Of white shell,
As perfect as a fan
In full half-moon . . . Next moment she's a hare:
The muzzle softens, rounds, goes dumb, and one
Tall ear dips, falters forward . . . Then,
Cross as switches, she's a great horned owl;
Two leafy tricorned ears reverse, a frown
Darkens her chalky visage, big eyes round
And round and stare down midnight.
                              There sits my cat
Mysterious as gauze,—now somnolent,
Now jocose, quicksilver from a dropped
Thermometer. When poised
Below the sketched ballet-
Dancers who pirouette upon the wall,
Calmly she lifts the slim
Boom of her leg, what will
The prima ballerina next
Perform?—Grace held in readiness,
She meditates, a vision of repose.

LIGNUM VITÆ

There in Bologna eighty saints are lodged
    On pedestals, in rows up
        The vaulted ceiling, till
            Heads meet at the top
                Of the hall.

Statues can wither like a blighted tree,
    The hand holding the pen suffers
        Dry rot, and a mantle embroidered
            So skillfully
                On oak

Disappears. Indeed, it is our loss
    Not to have lived five hundred years
        Ago, when in their vigor
            These figures were all
                One color.

A controversy now in black and white,
    The restored saints look down: one's right
        Hand is clean new pine,
            Another's torso
                Speckled

As a mosaic. Near the end is an old man
    Reading a new book; his robe
        Flows yet from broad shoulders
            Without break
                Or stain.

FOR A FLORENTINE LADY

I

At death's door: how is it—
On the edge of that old mountain, looking out
Through windows of a darkened villa
On and on, far across Florence? Mist—
Insatiable and dull—
Hoods the ground, and those
Loved and clean-cut forms go shapeless,
Dim. Dear Lady,
Can we then help you move
Through realms of mist
By seeing you so clear,
Who greeted us erect and sure?

II

At death's door: how was it—
From the final edge of suffering, looking back
On all the sunlit, terraced years,
Back and back, far across Europe? Death—
Insatiable and cruel—
Stabbed the air, and those
Loved and clean-cut forms went shapeless,
Fell. Dear Lady,
Could we have helped you move
Through realms of dark
By seeing you so clear,
Who greeted us erect and sure?

CITY AFTERNOON

Far, far down
The earth rumbles in sleep;
Up through its iron grille,
The subway, black as a chimney
Sweep, growls. An escalator rides
On dinosaur spines
Toward day. And on beyond,
Old bones, bottles,
A dismantled piano, sets
Of Mrs. Humphrey Ward all whirl
In the new disposal unit; above
Its din, apartments are tenanted
Tight as henhouses, people roosting
In every cupboard. Eighty stories
Up, pigeons nest on the noise
Or strut above it; higher,
The outcast sun serves its lean meat
Of light.

The whinnying
Of Venetian blinds has ceased: we sit
Invisible in this room,
Behind glass. In a lull,
A chance abatement of sound, a scalping
Silence, far
Down we hear the Iron
Maiden whisper,
Closing upon her spikes.

PORTRAIT OF THE BOY AS ARTIST

Were he composer, he would surely write
A quartet for three orchestras, one train:
After the penny-whistle's turn, he might—
With ten bull fiddles purring the refrain—
Dub in a lion to outroar the night.

Were he a painter, he would loose such bolts
Of color as would scare the sun, abash
Rainbows: a palomino-coated colt
Gallops on every speckled plain: a gashed
Knee bleeds rubies: frogs are emerald.

Were he a poet with the gift of tongues,
He'd scale the Andes in a metaphor,
Race Theseus in the labyrinth, among
Larks and angels act as troubadour,
For Daniel Boone shout at the top of his lungs.

Clear-eyed he sallies forth upon the field,
Holding close to his ear the shell of the world.

HOME LEAVE

With seven matching calfskin cases for his new suits—
Wife and three children following up the plank—
The Colonel shepherds his brood on board.

As the band pumps out "Arrivederci
Roma," the airman's apple
Face bobs over the first-class rail;
Across the watery gap, Sicilian
Crowds like lemmings rush at the narrowing pier.

Poised on the balls of his feet, the athlete
Goes below. Headwaiters
Screen him with menus; sommeliers
Approach on the double; corks pop to the creaking
Of timbers, while he dreams
Of winning every ship's pool.

Florid, the airman bunts
Favors around the dance floor: sky-blue-pink
Balloons doze on the air. It is the Captain's
Dinner; haloed in streamers, he romps
With a Duchess and wins
At Musical Chairs.

Later, on the boat deck, laced
Tight as a hammock by Irish
Whiskey, the athlete nuzzles the nurse. Collapsed
Like a tent around her, he rolls
With the ship.

After breakfast, the children on deck, New York
Near, balling his fists, the hero
Turns on his wife:
He hits out as if to do her honor.
With seven matching calfskin cases for his new suits—

Wife and children following down the plank—
The Colonel shepherds his brood ashore.

In forest-green sportcoat and desert brogans, he passes
Through Customs like quicksilver. His wife
Is heavily veiled; her three
Children follow like figures in effigy.

TRAMONTANA

Down from the north,
Clearing the hill's
Snow-topped shoulder,
Lashing the pale
Brittle grass,
The wind wheels.

Skimming the land
Low, like a sickle,
Shaking the trees
Barren that feel
Its vehement breath,
Taunting the bells'
Tranquil high
Calm as they peal
Notes like moons,
The wind growls
In mock singsong.

Arguing all
Day, all night
Plaguing, the dull
River of sound
Rises, fills
Our being, and mind
Taut as a sail
Snaps: in its
Continual bellow
We choke, drown;
The wind kills.

SIROCCO

Wind? This is no wind
Jaunty or wild like the others—
A substance buffing the skin—

This is a toad's wind:
Cantankerous and dull,
Irresolute, our brains

Are waterlogged; we quarrel
Spitting out yellow dust,
Ugly as puffballs

In the mustard-colored day;
Slack as a toad, our bleached
Land shimmers under its brassy

Sky. Amphibian green,
The warm consumptive air
Lowers, and will not turn

Inside out to keen and blow!
Fruit rots upon the vine;
The heart may start to mildew,

Rage take us by the throat,
Blood scald the eye until,
Stifling, we fall apart

Down to a lesser world.
This wind that hates the mind
Squats on till all is soiled.

MISTRAL

Percussive, furious, this wind
Sweeps down the mountain, and
Under its pennon of skirling air
Blows through each red-tiled house as if
Nothing were there: Mistral,
Quartz-clear, spread-eagle,
Falls on the sea.
Gust upon gust batters
The surface—darkening blue—
Into a thousand scalloped fans. Where
Shall our noontime friends,
Cicada, hummingbird,
Who stitched the air with sound and speed,
Now hide? All rocks, islands, peninsulas
Draw near, hitch up their chairs,
Companions in this clearer, clean
Air, while inland fields are stripped of soil.
As I start home, a coven
Of winds is let loose at every corner;
Alone in a howling
Waste, figurehead sculptured in air,
Bent low, deafened, I plunge
On, blind in the eye of the storm.

BALLADE OF THE INVENTORY: IN PROVENCE

Crying havoc through its recumbent
Oval mouth, the chandelier
Is, from below, a virulent
Iron mask; to one less near,
Indifferent, it becomes a mere
Distasteful fixture, number nine
Marked on the inventory here,
While the wind harries the great pine.

Item: one terrace with cement
Flooring, a locked armoire, five clear
Panes—*en guillotine*—a bent
Brass curtain rod, nine rings, a fear
Of things unlisted, a chiffonier
That teeters; two sponge racks, one tine
Missing; all form a lavaliere—
While the wind harries the great pine—

Or silken noose. What treasure spent,
What pride of possession, on this gear
Dusty, dimmed, impermanent,
Provisional. When nothing's dear
To anyone alive, a queer
Mélange remains. The sweet woodbine
Flaunts from a wall its green revere,
While the wind harries the great pine.

Etched poet of Provence, veneer
Peeling from your frame, we drink this wine
To do you honor. Could you but hear,
While the wind harries the great pine!

THE GALLERY

Into an empty cube
We step: the gallery,
Hung with ivory walls, lies still
As a squash court foundered in depths of sea.
Like players entering, we stare
Above the horizon line to where
Each opulent canvas, back to wall,
Confronts the room.
                              And then gaze on till sight
Flickers, and vision swims
In an emulsion of color, till down
Their cones of intervening air
The chipped-glass fragments form and blur.
Paintings upon four walls—nothing alive
But painting. When we have gone,
Pictures in their magnificence remain,
Tranquil as spring looking in at an open window
On an empty room.

L'ILE DU LEVANT: THE NUDIST COLONY

All the wide air was trawled for cloud
And then that mass confined in a gray net
And moored to the horizon. Bowed

Down, the golden island under
A dull sky was not at its best; its heyday
Is when the heat crackles, the sun

Pours like a boiling waterfall
On matted underbrush and thicket, on
Boulder, dust; and, over all,

Cicadas at their pastime, drilling
Eyelets of sound, so many midget Singer
Sewing machines: busy, then still.

Landing beyond a thorny curve
We climbed down to the colony, extended
On its plot of beach. In the sudden swerve

Of every eye, they saw as one,
These Nudists on vacation, half their days
Prone, determined as chameleons

To match the ground beneath. At ease
Within a sandy cage, they turned to stare
Up at us clad identities

Who came to stare as openly
As if we too had railings fore and back
And the whole mind of a menagerie.

Such freedom of the flesh, if brave,
Lacks subtlety: a coat of sunburn can
Be badly cut. Well-tailored love

Not only demonstrates but hides,
Not only lodges with variety
But will keep private its dark bed.

We rose: below us golden-brown
Bodies of young and old, heavy and lean,
Lay beached upon the afternoon.

While water, casual as skin,
Bore our departing boat, we saw a form
In relief against the rocky line

And stood to wave farewell from our
World to his, even as charcoal dusk
Effaced his lazy semaphore.

THE TRIUMPH OF TIME

         . . . Mounted on its triumphal chariot, Earth,
Shawled with the changing seasons, casts them off
In execution of a solemn dance:

Valleys the snow has leveled sink with spring
And hills start upward on a wave of green,
Warm winds sweep down on fallow pastures . . . How
Easily summer conquers: liberal,
It broods upon the world as a trapeze
Hangs poised above its long trajectory.
Autumn: a crazy hunter comes to poach
Inflaming all upon a zigzag path
Magenta, tangerine—the woods are torn
Asunder. Soon an old man whose mackintosh
Flaps about narrow flanks, will quit the house
And, hourglass in hand, check the sundial.
Old Doge, old Cupid, the sun at your time of year
Is pale as death;—and is it death that comes,
Darkening the wind?
         Although the dance would seem
To have reached its end, still clockwise earth will swing,
In each triumphant season witnessing
How this, this temporal dance, breaks from eternal love. . . .

THE TRIUMPH OF CHASTITY

Over the plain two dark
Equestrian figures pound
Charging full tilt at spring;
Behind them burnt-over ground,
A desolate panel stretches,
A long dun scarf unwound.

The taller, Cavalier
Hatred, his horny gut
Wild with the heat of their ride
Spurs onward, faster yet
Must he race his mighty Arab
Stallion; upon her jennet

Sidesaddle, stride for stride,
Gallops the Lady, fleet
Ambition; her sallow hair
Streams on the wind like light,
Cold as a cameo
Her face. They sow a great

Swathe of the plain with dust;
On, on he presses. Now,
Mantles like bellying sails,
They scud at the wood, and so
Storm forward till he reins in,—
Midnight upon his brow,

Caparisoned in jet,
Harness, panache of black
Spume-flecked, his stallion's eye
Encrimsoned;—they rein back
To their haunches the quivering steeds
At the brink:—Scrub, tamarack,

Meadows defoliate,
Autumnal. They who have
Outrun the spring, now halt
To seek as in a cheval
Glass one eternal face.
Each stares at his own self-love.

THE TRIUMPH OF LOVE

As from some grand
Venetian ballroom ceiling
Veronese's cupids
Gaze
Down, ringed
About the cupola,
Coronas of bright hair
Encircling them with light, suspended
There, clipped sturdy wings
Folded, chin in hand
Or holding tight the attic balcony which like
The top rung of a ladder wells
Dizzily above us who look up,
Heads thrown back, craning, seeking our
Reflected stare:

So toward the sleeping child do we
Converge,
Eyelids lowered and look down,
Once more so moved that all
Space dwindles
And the Palace walls
Are scaled to inches by our deepening love.

THE TRIUMPH OF DEATH

Illusion forms before us like a grove
Of aspen hazing all the summer air
As we approach a new plateau of love.

With disks of light and shade, vibration of
Leaf-candelabra, dim, all-tremulous there,
Illusion forms before us like a grove

And bends in welcome: with each step we move
Nearer, quick with desire, quick to dare.
As we approach a new plateau of love,

New passion, new adventure wait above
And call to our drumming blood; all unaware
Illusion forms before us like a grove

In a mirage, we reach out to take Love
In our arms, compelled by one another's stare.
As we approach a new plateau of love

The aspen sigh in mockery: then have
We come this way before? Staining the air,
Illusion forms before us like a grove
As we approach a new plateau of love.

THE TRIUMPH OF PRIDE

Not to retain,
Not to let go;
Not to approve—

Even of the blue heron
That soars and is gone—
Of anyone

Giving pleasure or pain—
Flown away so
Quickly, like love.

THE TRIUMPH OF TRUTH

Speaking out of a clear sky
I greeted two people at once; perhaps my eye
Saw less the real than the imagined figure.
These two repassed, rhythmically, like a fan,
Or like two dancers swaying
Apart, then eclipsing the other.

In an old painting Truth is drawn
In triumph by two elephants: a woman
Holding a great sword and a golden book,
While all around her, kings, philosophers,
And poets in her train
Nod and debate again.

How the rude sun has bronzed their skin!
See how her jeweled book reflects the inner
Light of their noble faces, of their crowns.
Truth's jet-black broadsword shudders over all,
An iron ruler poised,
That suddenly may sweep down.

Out of a clear sky Art speaks
The truth; two dancers separate and mix;
Each of us is an atoll whose protective
Shell is hard. But, a true mariner,
Art looks far out, and Truth
In triumph rides, with Love.

OUT FISHING

We went out, early one morning,
Over the loud marches of the sea,
In our walnut-shell boat,
Tip-tilting over that blue vacancy.

Combering, coming in,
The waves shellacked us, left us breathless, ill;
Hour on hour, out
Of this emptiness no fish rose, until

The great one struck that twine-
Wrapped flying-fish hard, turned and bolted
Off through the swelling sea
By a twist of his shoulder, with me tied fast; my rod

Held him, his hook held me,
In tug-of-war—sidesaddle on the ocean
I rode out the flaring waves,
Rode till the great fish sounded; by his submersion

He snapped the line, we lost
All contact, north, south, west, my adversary
Storms on through his world
Of water: I do not know him: he does not know me.

DEAD TOUCAN: GUADELOUPE

Down like the oval fall of a hammer
The great bill went,
Trailed by its feather-duster body
Splat on cement.
His mates fell out of countenance,
All listened, shivering in the sun,
For what was off, amiss:
In his pretend haven under a flame tree
The agouti crouched, chewed on his spittle, shook,
The porcupine rolled in his box, the parakeets
Chattered regrets,
Knowing something was wrong in their hot Eden:
That their king had followed his heavy fate to earth;
And his superb
Accomplishment,
His miracle of balance,
Had come to nothing, nothing. . . .
A beak with a panache
Chucked like an old shell back to the Caribbean.

TROY WEIGHT TAKEN

We do not need to comb
Arkansas to find
Rubies; loneliness
Vanishes in this crystal-
Clear actual air,
And one by one makes one.
Love tempers us, and every
True embrace is carved
In ivory; lasts; although
My eyes are shut, I learn
Each golden day that golden
Moorings hold me home.

A LETTER FROM THE CARIBBEAN

Breezeways in the tropics winnow the air,
Are ajar to its least breath
But hold back, in a feint of architecture,
The boisterous sun
Pouring down upon

The island like a cloudburst. They
Slant to loft air, they curve, they screen
The wind's wild gaiety
Which tosses palm
Branches about like a marshal's plumes.

Within this filtered, latticed
World, where spools of shadow
Form, lift, and change,
The triumph of incoming air
Is that it is there,

Cooling and salving us. Louvers,
Trellises, vines—music also—
Shape the arboreal wind, makes skeins
Of it, and a maze
To catch shade. The days

Are all variety, blowing;
Aswirl in a perpetual current
Of wind, shadow, sun,
I marvel at the capacity
Of memory

Which, in some deep pocket
Of my mind, preserves you whole—
As wind is wind, as the lion-taming
Sun is sun, you are, you stay:
Nothing is lost, nothing has blown away.

A CONVERSATION

For Isak Dinesen

As we stood on the crushed stone
Of the drive, it was as if
A spring landscape unrolled
Between. Colors deep
As gems—the tapestry,
Intricate and rich,
Of a lifetime. I was
Assumed into this world;
These emblematic hues
Shone like vintage wine:
Jet—that contains darkness
For those who have known the worst;
Beige—parchment-colored,
On which a burning glass
Etches the mind's runes;
Turquoise—that mood of green
And blue, field and sky—
Blending, to stand out.
Artist and woman moved there
Each in her separate light,
Clear-cut against a silver
Background of dream—all
Colors blend in silver,
A molten gong—whose full
Resonance an artist
Brocades upon the soul.

ON GALVESTON BEACH

The sky was battened down
Low all around us. We stood up
Into a sea of air,
First comers to this Sicilian element,
Prospectors motionless in a bowl of blue.

Down-at-mouth at the rim,
The barely-breathing sea
Neighbored flat sand; it waited
As a pier does for some sightseer
Of horizons to wander out.

If the sky is indeed a bowl
Pressed over us by a huge hand,
We have fellow creatures everywhere:
Sand in its patient minuteness,
That lean duck, his neck a hook, bobbing for fish,
Or those great mushrooms of the Gulf,
Jetsam jellyfish, in whose gills
Lie strands of aquamarine;
Their lives, so humpbacked and so white,
Resemble death. We stand awhile and watch
Waves worry them toward shore,
Before striking out in their sea.

ON SLEEPING TOGETHER

Day becomes explicit. From this shared
Warmth we grew into together here in bed,
Concave as a hammock, we are all one piece
At the moment of waking: is that my arm, or his?
Still linked and folded, slowly we withdraw
Selves and bodies from our world of sleep.
Caught in silhouette, heroic figures
Dim in the toils of darkness, but now responding
To the bravura of conch shell and drum,
Alive, we wake; waking, we separate,
With ceremony rise to greet the morning.

A NEAR-PANTOUM FOR A BIRTHDAY

At my Grandmother's life I look,
In this my fiftieth year of age,
Not a recluse, like her, not dark,
Withdrawn; for love is my stage.

In this my fiftieth year of age,
I'll figure out my place, and not
Withdraw, for love is my stage;
Loving and loved in this green spot,

I'll single out my place, not
As she the suburb of despair
(Loving and loved in this green spot)
Who breathed the shadows of the air.

As she—the suburbs of despair,
The cold body, the cold heart,
Who breathed the shadows of the air,
Denying love, kept all apart.

The cold body, the cold heart!
May this next decade see my warmth
Preserving love in every part;
Let me be held in my love's arms!

May these next years contain my warmth—
At Grandmother's thin life I look—
Let me hold love, then, in my arms,
Not a recluse, all quick, not dark.

THE LACE MAKER

Needle, needle, open up
The convolvulus of your eye,
I must come upon it quick
Or my thread will die.

Night is settling down outside,
My sallow candle seems to thin,
But I must weave this laddered thread
To nest each rare space in.

It is dark. Darkness plaits a scarf
Over my eyes. Can finger sprout
Eyes at the tip to guide its work?
Each evening, I go out

To Sainte Gudule—if I can see
Needlepoint of aspiring stone,
The window's rose embroidery
Trained like a trumpet upon Heaven,

Then I may live; but if my sight
Narrows toward death, a black-avised
Gargoyle will jut out, grinning there,
Exulting in that swirling mist.

THE CRANE CHUB: BARBADOS

Darling,
I learn
The full
Value
Of you
Again,
Savoring
The Crane
Chub,
Who idles,
Mates,
And dies,
Near one
Single
Reef
Just off
St. Philip
Parish;
He loves
His own,
Is of
A flesh
So rare
He must
Be eaten
Just
Within
The hour.
As your
Absence
Goes so
Against
The tide—
Sun,
Love,
Wind—
I now

Partake
Of Crane
Chub:
And oh
His essence
Is
Less rare,
Bitter,
Within
The flaw
Of your
Not being
Here.

THE LOVERS OF DELICATE THINGS

In Memoriam: W.P.D.

William and I
    Always want too much—
Want people to be porcelain
    But also willing;
Want the sensitive brain
    To triumph over the doings

Of the rough outside world.
    William and I
Seem to be obdurate, only
    We melt at the ring
Of the wrong number, at the
    Wild hope that everything

Is about to work
    Out according to our notions.
William and I
    Balk, check rein
On the stampede of those ponies
    Within us, strike out from our pain

With sharp hooves.
    It is better to be lonely
Than wrong, we think, or tasteless.
    William and I,
By giving up, give less
    Of ourselves to be hurt. By

Self-effacement, that Puritan
    Mask, do we conceal
The structure of our pride.
    We should have turned,
William and I,
    Away from power, have learned

That control is not needed
    Over others; simply of oneself, for
The lover of delicate things
    Can reach out and destroy
That to which he most clings—
    William!—Not I!

FOOTNOTE

Love is a great leveler.
Some of us
May fancy we have mastered desire—
Not likely; it's too imperious. For many
Love is a great
Barrier; some are ill
With fear of it. Few, really,
Have ever breathed its blue oracular air
Deep in their lungs. Love is a bell
That sounds and bodies forth the whole being.
We need own
So little: half a bed;
So much: hope that love is, will be
Love.

A STAND OF BIRCHES

For R. W.

Tall as if standing on jointed stilts,
This upright scaffolding,
These delicate laths
Firm to an altitude,
Much as seven-league boots might change
The gangling third son of a fairy tale
To one fit to win The Princess.

There is something in this silhouette
Of courtier and hobbledehoy,
Opposites strung like wire over the high
Paneling of the shoulders: impatient, cool;
A laconic herald;
Pan in an Ascot tie.

There is a gardener, too, stubborn, yare,
Whose work terraces the hillsides
Of language, possessed
By a nomad cast of mind that ranges
Furlongs over a landscape
Of solitude and distance.

Something that Holbein would have paused
Over informs this face:
He might have seen—
Painted on wood—the clean
Jaw and square brow, caught in those shadowed eyes
Vision that brought cathedrals higher, higher,
Lofty as there was stone for them;
All lit, all colored by
A heaviness of light,
New England Gothic chiaroscuro.

So, like a stand of birches, be briary, bend,
Touch earth, whip back to your high stance again.

DREAM OF A GOOD DAY

I dream of going in my outrigger canoe—
Buoyant, in balance upon each cobalt wave—
To follow the porpoise at his crescent play.

Or in my schooner, at its easy riding,
To imagine high in the crow's nest—which the ship
Sedately nods this way and that—a bed
Of crimson peonies, mine for the conceiving.

After, to wander alone the high wind-lanes,
With language all one's passion: its topsail
Scudding—then made fast: the poem strengthening,
Quieting down. . . . A day to dream of—
Then in the colloquial evening to come back to love.

SEA SCHOOL

This afternoon I swam with a school of fish.
Waiting in shallow water for the tide to change,
They swept at leisure through their green pleasance
Turning at will as one, or at some private
Signal all felt:
White and delicate, each one bedizened
By an ochre spot behind his sickle of gill,
Pale translucent fish they were, divided
By the hair-thin moustache line of backbone.

We plied our way along, taking our ease,
In concert, as a school
Feeling the flickering lozenges of light,
Chickenwire of sunlight grazing us
As we passed up and down under its stroke.
So for an hour, an age, I swam with them,
One with the rhythm of the sea, weightless,
Graceful and casual in our schoolhood,
Within our coop of light,
One with a peace that might go on forever. . . .
Till, of a sudden, quick as a falling net,
Some thought embraced them: I watched them go
Tidily over the reef where I could not follow.

MY DEAR, LISTEN:

If what may be
Is to turn—by grace, by craft, into poetry,
Is it not fine
That there are ten
Or more varieties
Of wild cherry,
And as for maples
There are multiple
Sorts that range
All over our ancient
American topsoil?
But then all
Of these fair trees
Know what species
They are—to what greatness
They may rise:
Reaching toward that
Preordained height
Their nature allows
And their fortune hallows.
Increasing, sowing
Seedpods and catkins
That a future forest
Of individualists
Will be assured.
In this mulligan world
Such family strictness
And integrity is
Profoundly moving;

More than other beings
An artist should keep
The pathway open
To his inward life,
To that native self

That must daily be fed,
Pondered and watered
If what might be
Is to turn—by grace, by craft—into poetry.

FOR KATHERINE ANNE PORTER

May 15, 1965

Madam, a siege
    Of heron
        Salutes you!

A spring of teal
    Flies criss-cross
        Through golden

Runnels of air, to say
    Luck, good omens!
        While a muster of peacock

Shows all-out
    Best wishes, a flight
        Of doves sends love;

A murmuration of starlings
    Builds up its iridescent
        Agreement

In trees, over fields; and then
    A watch of nightingales
        Flies in to do honor,—

And flies in through this fine
    Evening, to grace what all feel:
        An exaltation of larks!

ODE TO POSEIDON

Lines on a Grecian Urn Recently Acquired
by the Williams College Museum of Art

Well, hail, Poseidon! Old mariner who was caught
Between brothers—Zeus and Hades—but
    There you are, bent
    On sinking your new trident
Into the vitals of poor Polybotes,
Who rears back upon space as if a cot
    Waited; only his shield,
    A lion, will not yield,
But, twitching its black teardrop tail,
Glares out at us; Poseidon, hail!

On the vase's other side live three students
Dancing home, exams over, brains spent;
    Life in their heels, they clown
    The cobbled road on down
To celebrate. The central boy knows
What it is to want to *dance,* he fools and shows
    Them who is actor, they
    Are end men; so they play,
Lifting imagined wine in wassail
The students shout: Poseidon, hail!

One wed Poseidon from whom Pegasus
Sprang; no mean feat; many of us
    Know that most able horse,
    Whose love ran with the muse,
Could braid by the very rhythm of his hooves
The formal circlet this vase wears and weaves. . . .
    As to a theater-in-the-round,
    To lives, music, sound,
How well this winejar brings us in!
Oh, navigator, hail! Poseidon!

Vermont Poems: A Cycle

MOTHS IN WINTER

The sun,
Pied Piper this winter day,
Slants warmth in,

And up their glass-
Sheer barrier a moth
Flotilla sculls,

Tissue-paper-
Thin, shell-wings open,
As if there were

A life of days
Ahead; they sway there
Upon black ice,

While night deepens.
Colorless dancers, they long for
The shimmering neon

Inside, like divas
Drawing their wing-capes
Around them, as

Palmed against winter,
White magnets on that darkness
Of death, they falter.

Cold is the dancer.

THE SNOW HOLE

This morning early we came straight out of the house,
Over the saddle of the nearest ridge
To catch up with a logging road,
Then off, cross-country on our own,
On to the edge of landscape
To visit the sun.

We look ahead—ash and pine
Bristle over their summit.
The air is colder. As we climb
The sun bobs and treads ether.
Across the valley, down their great otter slide,
Utility poles are pegged one after one.

Then at the top,
Our heads against the sky,
We see what folk tale promised:—a cleft, a seam
Of purple whiteness nailed to earth,
Sealed off from light
By barricades of stone: a deaf white shaft.
This snow will never melt. Chilled through
By now, we touch the world.

TOWN MEETING TUESDAY

Our roadside trees seem to be gathering
Their forces; just the last few days they've changed
From hibernation to life—can they feel spring
A month ahead of time? Is their sap flowing

Already? Something processional in their bearing,
A flexing of boughs, so gray and strict all winter,
An implied fullness sign this lane of tree
On tree's covenant with spring—rose, purple, sepia.

Vermont Poems: A Cycle

A RUNE FOR C.

Luck? I am upset. My dog is ill.
I am now in that gray shuttling trains go in for;
The sky clouds, it is hard to believe dawn will

Ever show up.—I look for omens:
Not birds broken, not Fords lashed around trees,
But some item showing that fate is open. . . .

Sometimes, far, far down in the magical past
Of us all, in something that stutters, something that rises,
There is an intimation of luck just

Swinging over our way: a cat's paw loose
In the banister, a long train run, and then,
Square and oil-shambled, blue between elms, the caboose!

LOOKING UP AT LEAVES

No one need feel alone looking up at leaves.
There are such depths to them, withdrawal, welcome,
A fragile tumult on the way to sky.
This great trunk holds apart two hemispheres
We lie between. . . . Like waterlilies,
Leaves fall, rise, waver, echoing
On their blue pool, whispering under the sun;
While in this shade, under our hands the brown
Tough roots seek down, lily roots searching
Down through their pool of earth to an equal depth.
Constant as waterlilies we lie still,
Our breathing like the lapping of pond water,
Balanced between reflection and reflection.

Vermont Poems: A Cycle

ON FALLING ASLEEP IN A MOUNTAIN CABIN

We climbed together up to our mountain cabin,
Into a wooden room,
To live with the squirrels for one night.
Crickets clack-clacked, a mouse skittered;
Even the trees had disappeared, leaning to rest
On the deserted dark.

We too lay down. . . .
Under the single bulb the shadows rocked,
Our breath ballooned in the cold;
The icebox whirred: an outboard motor
Propelled us on, nearer the shoals of sleep.

One son dropped off, his faun's eyes
Leafy in the wavering light, the other lay
Brooding over a book; night lobbed
A dog's bark two miles up.
Our pine cabin was cool with the next season.
A short portage from home, we were deep in fall;
Summer, below, clear as a millpond lay—
That green expanse where we had dreamed all day.

LANDSCAPE, DEER SEASON

Snorting his pleasure in the dying sun,
The buck surveys his commodious estate,
Not sighting the red nostrils of the gun
Until too late.

He is alone. His body holds stock-still,
Then like a monument it falls to earth;
While the blood-red target-sun, over our hill,
Topples to death.

Vermont Poems: A Cycle

DEATH OF A VERMONT FARM WOMAN

Is it time now to go away?
July is nearly over; hay
Fattens the barn, the herds are strong,
Our old fields prosper; these long
Green evenings will keep death at bay.

Last winter lingered; it was May
Before a flowering lilac spray
Barred cold forever. I was wrong.
                    Is it time now?

Six decades vanished in a day!
I bore four sons: one lives; they
Were all good men; three dying young
Was hard on us. I have looked long
For these hills to show me where peace lay . . .
                    Is it time now?

RUNNING INTO EDGAR BELLEMARE

In my fool seigneurial car
I came storming through dust, whirling around the corner:
Bang into skidding distance of skidding
Bellemare, his unfledged wife, four sorry
Towheaded chicks under five, in their Hupmobile.

It amounted to little more than *Plunk:*
Their eggshell auto crumpled. We sat on
And stared at this odd joining;
And then, unspanning, took off again
About our business. The big car pawed the road
Less mettlesomely. The Bellemares
Went on back down to find a spare fender
At Hawkes' junkyard; all of them to huddle—
Sheltered by that fender—a little longer,
Armored for life by a breastplate frailer than wishbone.

A FEW DAYS AGO

That dark adventure was a tree,
A beldame spruce, inside whose trunk
The sap flowed secretly

Threaded to what had gone before;
Each mood or prospect had kinship
Through that slim corridor

From taproot to leaf filament.
I found myself enclosed within
The experience. It lent

Its temper to those days, until
It was all over.—Relieved,
I moved again at will

Without that darkness ruling me,
Nor swept along in the winey sap
Of that wind-shaken tree.

What will follow? Things come upon
Us unexpectedly. I wonder
What image or condition

Will bind my next fortnight together:
The stately rising of an elm
Or sullen golden straw?

Vermont Poems: A Cycle

LATE NOVEMBER WINDOW

A light turns on among the trees, it glows
Through a forest of filetted bones; a lamp
Shimmers just over the carapace of the hill;
Then fades, blurs; waxes, glows.

Stars are not bright enough
To warn if the clouds reel
Awash in the firmament,
Or what ne'er-do-well in the dead
Of night is out hunting the living.

Under the phantasmagoria of sky
Our earth lies black, secret; only that brilliance
Waiting to dazzle a stag, to flash
Death in his eyes.—Oh, but that light
Has cleared our arc of trees; is it then simply
The moon out jacking deer; and fear and I?

THE DRESSMAKER'S DUMMY AS SCARECROW

On the hillside's upper garden a dressmaker's dummy
Is set among carrot and cress.
No longer can she swivel
In rooms that faces have paneled, eyeballs lit,
Informing stuff with her articulate line;
For an outside world she now stands sentinel
Against the crows, the shy
Foraging rodents who patter
By crisscross paths nearer by.

There is at times a blindspot in our view
When one sees nothing, is nothing, cannot see
How one has drifted here;
                    At that breaking point, one is out of place
As a dressmaker's dummy left there under the sky:
Outside, she is her livery, but changed,
Apart, surrounded by garden; the fern
At the end of perspective
Reaches now to her shoulder;
The moles are wiser and the crows are older;
She may, or she may not, outlast the winter—
The spring may find her still, and grow towards her.

Vermont Poems: A Cycle

A NIGHT PICTURE OF POWNAL

For J. F. K.

Thanks to the moon,
Branches of our trees are coral
Fans, cast on the lanky snow
Which, crusted though,

Takes impressions
As Matthew Brady's eye received
The desperation of Civil War;
He was its retina

And watched history
Rise and set. Above its kilt
Of steel-blue air the moon turns,
A circle leans

To stare down fissures
Of space to that black forest set
Like matchsticks on the white hillside;
All sound has died.

Our apple tree
Prints its own photograph, its strong
Branches espaliered on the snow
Fading, will not go

From our minds, the clean
Etching of dark on white, each detail
Tuned to the whole; in its precision
Enduring as bone.

What we have seen
Has become history; tragedy
Marks its design upon the brain—
We are stained by its stain.

Vermont Poems: A Cycle

LEANING INTO LIGHT

Our hibiscus, larch,
    Marjoram, cork tree,
       Dandelion seek
         Light—
      A dull day
    Has them listless, olive-
Green, no sap running,

As I in a bad
    Time am in shadow,
       Uncertain. But then
        Light,
      Like a prophet,
    Calling them forth
To grow in the sun's great

Eye—as wisteria
    Climbs toward day—
       They revive; I have known
        Light
      Too, a presence
    One turns round to face,
Leans into and joins.

Away

RETURNING TO STORE BAY

      Coming back to this generous island—
Shore, harbor, beach—
Is to leave behind images blown
Like cats through a shadow alley,
      And the feel of cement in the teeth . . .

      Returning to Store Bay
One comes back to the circular sound
Of wind whacking the scrolled
Water, the vast contest
      Of undertow and surf;

      To the savage ironing
Of breezes, rolling on out, stropping,
Whaling, pulling back in, the water
Huge in some artisan hand;
      Surf and wind are round.

      —In a ferryslip, wings
Of brown paper from a subway
Kiosk play hopscotch, stretch out
In gutters of that town whose
      Sidewalks abrade the throat.—

      Coming back to this bay
Is to meet again the guffawing
Ocean, is to dance, dimensional,
Hewed out by wind, in the round,
      Alive in the muscular sea.

A LETTER FROM LITTLE TOBAGO

This feeling of being alone,
>> Visiting all these birds who live here—
>> Who are in some way our hosts—
>> And who know that when night
>> Falls they will be alone,

Is moving. About that unquarried quarry,
>> Over its flat north rock-face,
>> White Red-Billed Tropic
>> Birds slant and ride out the air
>> On their paper-cutter-thin tails—quarry

Of nothing because too rare; silent—
>> They swoop, balance, rise, then
>> Are thrown back to their grassy cliff,
>> On their own; their delicate bone-
>> White tails the slimmest of fans. Silent

The path we ascend; roots like lanyards
>> Or narrower, saplings give us a hand,
>> And we come up into birdsong—our guide
>> Long part of this jungle, we two others now
>> Entering: woodspeople. Lanyard

Trees thicken, stand taller; we are right
>> In the forest, tuned to each bird, to noting
>> The least vibration of color
>> In this deep leaf-padded green-
>> Yellow strangeness; careful, we move right

Toward a courtly groaning, the Birds
>> Of Paradise' showy courting; they
>> Display, they let drift down that
>> Underwing gossamer-fall, that
>> Yellow smoke, something no other bird

Away

Has. Then Motmots, Yellowtails, Jacamars,——we
    Have never seen such profusion
    Before; any branch
    Can be used by the Cocrico
    As pedestal, which he takes to; we

Have lived two whole hours alone
    On the birds' own island. We have saluted
    Them by being quiet, like sensible trees;
    By being in view, they have saluted back. The
    Birds of Paradise honored us: we saw them alone,

Perched in those thickening leaves,
    Which blur, which interrupt sight;
    Now all around us birds, rocks, trees
    Know we are going, letting them
    Be, to nest as they will in their leaves.

We have boarded our dinghy and left,
    Jounced back over
    The gray mill wheel of water;
    Forest wisdom opens on mystery;
    Mystery roofs the shy lives we have left.

Away

VOYAGE AUTOUR DE MA CHAMBRE

The Harkness Pavilion

Earliest of all rectangles,
      I see from my bed
A slab of building, gray out there,
      Then rose-dusted; then it's whacked
      By light, as the Arab
Sun hits it pell-mell.—A lateen
      Rig among shadows.

Becalmed in my bed,
      I wait out the tidal hours;
Nurses, from their corridor-jetty,
      Ferry forth and back
      Their soundless
Emollient nostrums; a silent
      Bell-buoy nudges the rocks

Which lie like cranked hospital
      Cots among shallows, teethed . . .
Beyond my bulrush bed, the eraser
      Sun rubs out buildings; over it an Arch-
      Bishop, tall in gauze mitre, white gown,
Leans. A Prophet? A Martyr?
      He looks down.

Away

LUKE, CAPTIVE

Pacing his two
Footage that way,
Rearing up, leaning this,
So that no interstice
Would be missed, Luke
Studied his prison-
Seminar again, on the chance . . .
The kinkajou,

Or honey bear,
Is a gentle, trilling,
Nocturnal creature,
Soft cinnamon-furred,
Who would house
If he could
In his Central American
Forest; Luke would

Like to.
—What is a tree
To an animal? A
Direction? Camouflage?
A city-state?
Solid in air
It branches, and dawn
Or noon is next door and there.

Now in his huge
Cage, in dusky
Day asleep, through velvet
Night he courses
From one jungle
To another,
In a dark sweet
Withdrawal of imagination.

Away

WILD GEESE FLYING

Aware at first only of the dust of sound
　Drifting down to us here in the yard,
　　I saw him look up, searching fathoms of air
　　As for tidings,
　　　Some urgent spirits' honking aloft:
　　　　Wild geese there—and my eyes strained after,
　　　　Into that azure,
　　　　　Then, *there* they were: *there*,
　　　　　　Flying in a straggle, so high, a wonder,
　　　　　　Glinting like wafers, silver fish-
　　　　　　　Scales in the sun, a
　　　　　　　　Strewing of foil confetti, yet aimed;
　　　　　　　The string of a kite's tail
　　　　　　　Dipping, being drawn
　　　　　　　　Through that gulf stream of air
　　　　　　　　　By their migrant passion;—at the edge
　　　　　　　　　Of sight I still found them. . . .
　　　　　　　　Then, abruptly,
　　　　　　　　Nowhere.

THE LONELY PIPEFISH

Up, up, slender
As an eel's
Child, weaving
Through water, our lonely
Pipefish seeks out his dinner,

Scanty at best; he blinks
Cut-diamond eyes—*snap*—he
Grabs morsels so small
Only a lens pinpoints them,
But he ranges all over

That plastic preserve—dorsal
Fin tremulous—*snap*—and
Another çedilla
Of brine shrimp's gone . . .
We talk on of poetry, of love,

Of grammar; he looks
At a living comma—
Snap—sizzling about
In his two-gallon Caribbean—
And grazes on umlauts for breakfast.

His pug-nosed, yellow
Mate, aproned in gloom,
Fed rarely, slumped,
Went deadwhite, as we argued on;
That rudder-fin, round as a

Pizza-cutter, at the
End of his two-inch
Fluent stick-self, lets his eyes
Pilot his mouth—*snap* . . .
Does his kind remember? Can our kind forget?

GOLD *BEYOND* GOLD

*For the Opening of the Rogers Collection of Greek Gold
at the Williams College Museum of Art*

"Emeralds are green *beyond*
Green; you look down into them
And see the *truth* of green."

This central wreath—over
Whose strawberry leaves Athena's
Heart-faced owl presides—

Is goldsmith genius, the Hellenes'
History in art. It is a wreath
Symbol for Alexander, whose giant

Dream of Empire—joining
Greece to Asia Minor—cut a swathe
Of conquest from a route of gold.

. . . Soon, lynx, panther, griffin, ram (Darius' treasure)
Flowered on earring, pendant,
Belt: creatures of Dionysus, images

Of predatory urgings, fears
Of an alloyed world,
Alive in gold.

Herakles' knot, that amulet
At center, frequently, of diadem,
Thigh band, foot bracelet, ring,

(A reef knot plain or garnet-studded,
Inlaid with any treasure)—this
Golden symbol of relationship,

They held, would heal
Wounds; deeper than this, it stands
For the grave, wild permanence of love.

CRYSTAL-CLEAR, DIAMOND-BRIGHT

As they had no ice in Tobago,
She thought it a blue shame
To see—as she cleaned up college
Rooms—all those steel-tinted ice-squares
Subsiding into drainwater. It shook her. So

She rolled tight
The rotund "cardboard-pak bag
Whose wet strength is
5 1/2 lbs"; lugging it with
Her—baby on hip—she
Waited at the Duke Street bus stop;
It dripped, but not much. When the bus
Hurtled up,
It clung cold to her side
Like treasure; while they stalled
In all that exhaust, she thought
About dryness in her village, Moriah,
And how only some miracle-
Magnet kept life
From falling off that

Toboggan hill.—At Main
The cool was damper. Then
Finally, out on Luck Street,
Propping open the door of
Her room—a chill still between it and her—
She was home, inside,
Alone—in a peace of crystal.

MERCEDES

Hopscotch
> Through patches
> Of light, a green-eyed
Dominican slanted
> From palm-frond street shadow in
To a job, to stay on, to be safer;
But by June, daubed soap on her mirror:
Mercedes de la Rosa está muerta

Mercedes had
> Worked Casuarina-long days:
> "San Francisco, San Francis-
> Co, San Fran . . ." written fifty-three
> Times . . . "In my grandmother's garden
Tomatoes grew, red whole
Hearts, we ate them; they said
> *'Mercedes de la Rosa is dead'* "

Dream-knives
> Cut out dolls—but I'll
> Help them—that leaf,
> Falling, is a dory . . .
> Chicago, Chicago;
Men: their pants
Pressed to the coil of a whip,
> Shoot billiard
> Eyes at me . . .
Merced es de la Rosa

I can hide my dolls, my
> Cuckoo clock, though his beak
> Orders me to dance;
Sequins, I glue gold pieces, I sew
Justice on chiffon,
All colors—as I whirl,
> They dance—how my body aches!

Away

     I must nail my cuckoo . . . The
Spinning mirror splinters:
    Mercy befits the Rose

Next day, duck with two heads,
Her radio quacked to itself; a needle
Slanted through the cuckoo's
    Heart; lint of chiffon
Rocked in Erzulie's breeze . . . "People
    Do strange sometimes," she had said,
    And,
Mercedes de la Rosa is dead

Away

AT MRS. ALEFOUNDER'S

Tobago

Not perched on the top of the hill
But established there, a nest
        Leaning into a blue
        Sky, this white and blue
House is an aviary; winds live outside
And in, not knowing the difference; still,

It is a house, not quite an aviary,
Though made of porches, windows,
        Weather, verandahs, open
        To all moods of air, opening
Out on trees standing apart
Like old friends . . . Save

For the one peacock, birds
Who arrive at this giant feeder
        Come in numbers. Grasping the tilt,
        Their table, they peck—swaying as the tilt
Sways—at that mash, plump
In bill. They are outdoors, but stirred

By terrace breezes . . . The stocky Anis—
Blacker than black—drive
        Roman-nosed beaks
        At their banquet, while slimmer beaks
Of Bananaquit, Woodpecker, and the dun
Or lilac Dove, or Tanagers, sky-

Blue, cloud-white partake. The Motmot's chest
Chestnut, cap azure, each delicate
        Morning coat irridescent, one handsome
        Jewel slotting the breast;—indeed handsome
Beyond belief, at tail's end twin prongs
Support an extra feather-inch, a test

Away

Nature has rarely passed . . . Cocricos scamper
Pheasant-heavy, purplish, a pink wattle
      As chin, body a sturdy
      Brown; for reasons of sturdy
Attraction, an undertail fan goes orange;
They loft to a plumtree and back, trample

Their provender . . . On this balcony or off
We are outside-within an aviary,
      Free in it;—then shadow
      Tucks itself underleaf, shadow
Seines birds away, ourselves also,
As night lowers over us its abrupt snuffer.

Away

ON BUCCOO REEF

For Carl

Walked by these black oak
Legs, my mermaid hand held,
I drifted three feet over
Our coral kingdom—masked—
In the gentle, slow life
Of the reef.

Led by this dry hand
Through currents, edged past red
Stinging coral, growing
As men grow, goggled, I watched
The violet mandarin whiskers
Of a triggerfish,

His mustachioed tail . . .
And parrot- and squirrel-
Fish, eyes large as coins;
Others—an emerald triangle—
Wreathe rock and are gone . . .
Grizzled by sun,

My mermaid hand held,
Alive underwater, I saw,
Masked, their open eyes . . .
I am walked back now
Up in to air
By these oak legs.

THE BLUE GARDEN

      Blue: aconite, deadly;
Iris, a grape
Hyacinth, or tulip
          Bulb lives deep
      Down under; in March
      They drill up through that frozen
         Turf.—
      Blue often reverts to magenta.

      Blue: larkspur
         Sets its annual
Poisonous
Sights at six feet;—each
Year the
      Delphinium, too,
         Kills lice;
And both revert to magenta.

      Blue: the delicate fringed
         Gentian is a rarity
         To be protected,
  As gentian
  Violet is either
         Elegance or tincture;
Still, these too can revert to magenta.

      Blue: cornflowers
         Secure in their August
         Field, like bachelors'
Buttons, asters—reliable
         As wheat—return
         For their violet season;
What tone is magenta?

      It must be autumn's
         Color: camouflage: white-
Tailed deer, red maples

Drying, that brown hawk diving
     Gray as a pellet: a hodgepodge
     Of pigment; middle
        Age has its own hue,
Which can easily revert to magenta.

     Even so, our yarn of blood
       Knits us together,
       Working
Its own narrative . . .
       This color may hold—blue
       As some eyes are—and not
    Revert, but keep cobalt, cobalt.

OTIS

"When King George the Fifth
Died, my cows were happy;
They needed just that sort
Of music to ease 'em down,
                    Same as a person."

Our two horses enjoy
Their separate, canopied four-
Poster stalls, with silvered
Wadding run to the ridgepole,
                    That Otis made them.

"Waltzes, and something soft,
Is what cows like for music;
Then they rest quiet . . ." His sheep,
Grooming the upper pasture,
                    Are belled for safety,

And their far cadence tolls
Summer's opulent hours—
While tallow fleeces thicken—
And winter's thinning days;
                    "We've had a cold

Spring for eighteen years
That hasn't failed us, it's
Based on quicksand: warm
Winters, and cool in May;
                    It never froze."

A wonder of nature—"wood
Splits well in cold weather"—
How things are, how things
Work, that is the study
                    Of a happy man:

"Keeping animals takes
Plenty of knowing; they have
Their ways, you just must think
Quicker than they do," Otis
　　　　　Said, knowing he did.

At Home

AT 79TH AND PARK

A cry!—someone is knocked
Down on the avenue;
People don't know what to do
When a walker lies, not breathing.

I watch, 10 stories high,
Through the acetylene air:
He has been backed up over;
Still, the accident

Is hard to credit. A group
Of 14 gathers; the fire
Department rains like bees,
Visored, black-striped on yellow

Batting, *buzz*—they clamber
Around that globule; somebody
Brings out a comforter
For shroud; a woman's puce

Scarf bobs, from my 10th-floor view,
Desperately; by the backed truck
An arm explains, hacks air
In desperation, though no

One takes much notice. As through
A pail of glass, I see—
Far down—an ambulance,
A doctor come; they slide

Away the stretcher . . . In minutes
The piston arm, the truck,
Puce, police, bees, group
All have been vacuumed up.

At Home

BEST OF SHOW

Wheatfields of chiffon,
Afghans are blown
Into the ring: spun-silk
Waterfall, while

Popeyed Chihuahuas
Toothpick about, each
Radar-cocked ear
Plucking news . . . Now

Golden as carp,
Pekingese waddling
On fins of fur,
Whelk tails, swim in;

Next, the Great Danes,
Brindle or pinto,
Sleek as wallpaper,
Enter

Before feathered
English
Setters, time on their
Point to snoot

Most poodles, those
Peacock, tonsured, bright-
Eyed balls of cotton-
Candy; and

Bassetts,
Paws whiter than sneakers,
Map ears their
Epaulettes; or

At Home

Weimaraners,
Coats silver
On bacon, yellow
Eyes sly; so different

From Huskies',
Whose Arctic
Look is a squint . . .
These breeds strut till,

Wheezing over its bow-
Legs, a lap
Dog trembles in:
Best of show!

TALKING TO ANIMALS

For Cary

When there are animals about, who else—
People aside—does one talk to?
They form an environment of ear and eye
Most finely adjusted to turns
Of mood: terror, humor . . .

The domesticated: cats and dogs
Speak freely, handle their own
Lives, adjust our natures
To theirs and back; as cattle—
Those enormous oblongs of good-

Will—did they state their strength,
Could smash a barn a day;
As ducks in their sewing circle
Wonder, wander, flapping their
Fluent tails; as a mare

Lumbers, an iron horse on the turntable,
Setting forth a fact, while her foal's eyes dance
Like legs. Smaller creatures: four
Inches of chipmunk tell hazard
From ruin as people can't . . .

Making oneself understood
To animals—as to people—
Is a question of tone of voice,
Of communication just
Right for that neighbor;

Perhaps of being inside
A hogan, or in the middle
Of anywhere, one's antennae out,
Like my Beaver Spirit who takes—deep
In his Eskimo ear—much wisdom from a loon.

SHELL

The strong delicate shell
      Of the body—shoulders
      Rising like music, subsiding,
Turning toward me like dawn—
      Arches, in warmth, a wave
      Fluted, and I rise up
To welcome the wash of the sea.

A small kettledrum, nacre,
      The slim clear heart-of-pearl
      That relays the
Ocean's tidal message,
      Meanwhile it secretes,
      As flesh does, rainbows—holds dawn in its
Curve—yet bears them within.

All these ivory breezes
      Indent the sea; and sea
      And wind thus form
A shell, or a vast scallop
      Of air and water; they meet
      Forming each other.
Shell warms; when warmed

It emerges from its resonant
      Depth, draws one to look
      Down to the whorled
Architecture of the human. Warmth is
      Kindled by touch. Into
      This scalloped world we are born:
Ourselves shaped by our white housing of skin.

At Home

FOR AN OLD FRIEND

H. F. Z. at ninety

At peace on your porch—
    The garden
    Smoldering under the dark
    Vigil of cypress and privet—

You tell me that,
    Free now
    From desire and surfeit, you
    Can see human emotion in scale:

An Alpine relief
    Map,
    Rainbow geometry, bells
    Lunging in the Campanile. . . .

This hullabaloo
    About life
    Is not my forte, you might
    Add, as I ask your blessing. . . .

Brushstrokes, this green
    Wisdom,
    A vine: sitting frail in your chair,
    Towering, dispensing light.

STILL LIFE: NEW ENGLAND

From that old cow in the field
　　　　A calf was born;
He struggles now to rise—
　　　　No, he cannot
Yet, on his tapestry legs;
　　　　The cow, crosshatched
With dirt, lice, underfed,
　　　　Her cud a sour
Lozenge in her throat
　　　　Rolls agate eyes.

Sheep with their earnest profiles
　　　　Vaguely pit
Their muzzles at the gate,
　　　　Wait to stampede;
If luck works for them, bars
　　　　Will slide by their neat
Feet; grass will surround
　　　　Them, camouflage
Through which they'll crop a path
　　　　All through green summer.

While the boar, in the strawyard
　　　　Of his excrement,
Tunnels, grunting through
　　　　Each four-walled day,
The cow lies in the field;
　　　　The calf she bore
Dies—. With what a spray
　　　　Of whiskers, the yellow
Barncat saunters forth,
　　　　Smells death, returns,

Prinks in the barn doorway . . .
　　　　The cow lurches
To her feet, in need of fodder,
　　　　Hocks trembling,
Ridgepole of hipbones slanting

Through her canvas hide
Sharp as a longhorn's skull;
She subsides—
Her eyes, agate no longer,
Thicken to rubber.

CARDINAL

With deep snow
        A fresh page
                Stretches
                Toward the tree-
        Line; within, a new page
Reflects the gray-white of

Ceiling; never flat,
        Snow rolls with the
                Earth's breathing—
                Slivers
        Of light, reflected,
Skate like grasshoppers

Over the whole white-
        Carpeted landscape,
                Or again, in gray
                Weather, blend into
        Dusk;—those matchstick
Trees out there, poled

Into snow, are characters
        Cutting their own shadow. My
                Page now has markings:
                Hieroglyphs of
        Talon, pen, shade,
Hoof range over this open

Country imprint it. On snow-
        Fall—as the white
                Magic between us
                Is signed—I see
        The cardinal's red cursive
Line, written on winter, writing to spring . . .

REGINA COELI

This early, the small birds' trudging notes;
Six stories high, a crane looms
     As in graceful blessing . . .
     Jaywalkers are Roman matadors,
     Charioteers drive taxis.

Past the *Palazzo di Giustizia,*
Its face being lifted, under reed awnings,
We race like dolphins through wet sound.

A new day starts up
     Through a halo of birdsong,
And I remember the *Pietà,*
She so clothed, he so naked; the withdrawn
     Young face dreaming of her old son.

     Vines branching up from each balcony,
     Flowering pots in each window, whittled-
Back plane trees shouting green;
Umbrella pines guarding old walls.

. . . My hand held to that warm cheek—
I thought of what hands were
To Michelangelo—they hold, they save;
The hand, the maker, steadiness of the heart
     —Son, my son—
Confirm direction.

The weathered church
     Jail-gray across the street,
     Wisteria everywhere
     Flowering upward
Over the lunging city—
     Pink socks on a Vespa volley off—
Our hands may be cardboard praise . . .
     Regina Coeli
     Free his youth,
     Give him grace to wake
     To a halo of birdsong!

FOR GENOVEVA FOREST DE SASTRE
AND FOR KITTY GENOVESE

> Haitian proverb: *"The pencil of God has no eraser."*
> Robert Burns: *"Man's inhumanity to man . . ."*

Is ineradicable; cruelty adds inches
To the Falange boot,
To brass-knuckled hatred
Of Genoveva's humankind.

Kitty, sensing the pad of feet, the jackknife,
Screamed up to those empty cubes
Where people, lacquered by television
Crime, were deaf. Each one.

How can I reconcile thoughts of
Kitty, Genoveva with myself—
One dead, one dying, one safe still,
At work on language?
If you *know* this sorrow, it breaks the heart
Apart like a split cabbage.

THE MIRROR

For David

The mirror reflects what it must reflect:
 A Bavarian room, hiking-shoe colored,
 The dirndl lampshade on its weighted
 Chain; sallow walls stare at that glass
 which holds all in place.
If this mirror, in its curlycued gold,
 Had a counterpart
 Across the room,
 They would—while Sunday bells toss high
 Alpine cadenzas—
See deeply. I look in your eyes,
 Reflections combatting,
 Mingling. Is the future shown there also,
 Also in place?

MAN WITH VIOLIN

For M. W.

Under a combed-pine ceiling, a maze,
 The man with violin
Tunes his thought and plays

Arpeggios in red flight. His heart's
 Busy, musical memory
Prompts us to set

Up a portrait of one
 Who knows his world, all delicate
Art's rivalry, and hurricane;

Who knows, with a farmer's true sense,
 The stance of a prime Jersey—
True music, true fond silence.

SECOND WIND

My son's house
        Up on our hill,
Looks out, over my shoulder;
Its barn-cabin being
        Takes to a scudding wind.

It looks away at land
        Roiling under white cover,—
Tree-banks massive as dinosaurs
Smoothing to field; snow squalls.
        Drummed by a wild wind

I look up at
        This edifice tuned
By twenty years green
Learning. Across the valley
        An iron flurry speaks.

As my son's house
        Looks far, it is
Seasoned, there; from this proud
Young life a seconding
        Wind breathes through me—

And I accept
        My autumn wandering,
Winter, June's
Skeleton summer . . . Now
        So blows, now, my second wind!

ALL THAT'S TO OTHERS PLEASING, I DISLIKE

All that's to others pleasing, I dislike;
 The whole world brings me ennui and grief.
 —Then, what do you enjoy?—I answer, brief:
 —When each opponent makes the fatal strike:

I like to watch blows of a sword fully
 On another's face, and vessels foundering:
 To be a second Nero would be pleasing,
 And that each lovely woman should be ugly.

Amusement and good cheer I cannot breathe:
 And melancholy's what I relish most:
 All day I'd gladly follow some tomfool,
 And pay my court to sorrow for a while,
 And slaughter all whom in my cruel thoughts
 I do slaughter, there where I find death.

Cino da Pistoia (1270–1336)

CHRISTINE TO HER SON

Son, of great fortune have I none
To make you rich: instead of gold,
Though, certain lessons I would bring
Up, if you'll give them a hearing.

From first youth, innocent and pure,
Learn to know what people are,
And so, by seeing what they're like,
Protect yourself from gross mistake.

Upon the destitute take pity,
Poor creatures you will naked see,
Give them assistance as you may!
Bearing in mind you too will die.

Love him who is a friend to you
And watch out for your enemy:
No one can have too many friends,
There is no minor enemy.

What serves the Lord do not discard
For a world overmuch enslaved:
The worldly go to meet their fate
And the enduring soul holds out.

Christine de Pisan (1364–?1431)

BALLADE: THE HOSTELRY OF THOUGHT

Across the forest of Delay,
By many a winding woodland route,
This present year, full eagerly,
Drawn by desire have I set out.
The aides that I dispatched have sought
To find me lodging in the city
Of Destiny, and take what ought
To satisfy my heart and me,
The goodly hostelry of Thought.

And I have marshaled forty bay
Steeds, for my officers have brought
Sixty or more all told—pray
God!—and baggage mules to boot.
If inns are wanting or all bought
Up, we will scatter readily;
Yet be it only for one night,
Whatever comes, I will essay
The goodly hostelry of Thought.

My ready funds I spend each day
In actions of some daring sort,
The which a jealous Fate who plays
Me cruelly takes in ill part.
But if my Hopes run high and straight,
And hold to what they promised me,
Such seasoned troops will I have wrought
I'll win, despite my enemy,
The goodly hostelry of Thought.

Prince, true heavenly deity,
Your grace I pray be my resort,
Until what I desire I see—
The goodly hostelry of Thought.

Charles d'Orléans (1391–1466)

THE CATS OF SANTA ANNA

So many cats so often multiply
 They number double the stars in the Great Bear:
 Cats we observe whose coats look entirely white,
 Black cats also, and calico cats are there;
Cats with tails, and other felines tailless:
 A cat with a camel's hump I'd like to see,
 Dressed up as monkeys sometimes are, in suits
 Of velveteen: can't you find one for me?
Let mountains take care, likewise, when about
 To be delivered, that they do not bring
 Forth a mouse, who, indeed, poor fellow,
 From such a gang could never save himself.
Housewife, I warn you, keep your mind and eye
 On the stewpot boiling at the back of the stove;
 Quick, look! One's run away with the *scallopine!*
   Now I'll add the refrain:
  Fully to praise this sonnet and commend,
  Its tail must resemble a cat's and have an end.

        Torquato Tasso (1544–1595)

THE ROSES OF SA'ADI

I wanted this morning to bring you a gift of roses,
But I took so many in my wide belt
The tightened knots could not contain them all

And burst asunder. The roses taking wing
In the wind were all blown out to sea,
Following the water, never to return;

The waves were red with them as if aflame.
This evening my dress bears the perfume still:
You may take from it now their fragrant souvenir.

     Marceline Desbordes-Valmore (1786–1859)

EL DESDICHADO

The dark one am I, the widowed, unconsoled,
Prince of Aquitania whose tower lies ruined,
My one star is dead, and my radiant lute
Renders only the black sun of Melancholy.

In the night of the tomb, oh, you, my consoler,
Give me back Pausilippo and the Italian sea,
The flower which delighted my desolate heart,
And the trellis where the vine and the roses marry.

Am I Eros or Phoebus, Lusignan or Biron?
My brow is still red with the kiss of the Queen;
I have dreamed in the grotto where the siren swims . . .

And twice have I, victor, crossed the Acheron:
Passing, in turn, on Orpheus' lyre
From the sighs of a saint to a fairy's cries.

Gérard de Nerval (1808–1855)

THE HIPPOPOTAMUS

The hippo, huge of abdomen
In darkest Java's jungle dwells,
Where from the depths of every den
More monsters snarl than dream can tell.

The boa comes uncoiled and hisses,
The tiger launches forth his roar,
The angry water buffalo sneezes,—
Quiet, he rests, or pastures, for

He fears nor kriss nor javelin,
He looks at man and never hides,
Unruffled, notes the Indian
Bullets rebounding from his sides.

A hippopotamus I am;
My basic certainty is this:
As nothing hurts the strongly armed,
Whole deserts can I range with ease.

Théophile Gautier (1811–1872)

TEA

Miss Ellen do, pray, pour the tea
Into this charming Chinese cup,
Where fishes all of gold take up
Their quarrel with a scared pink beast.

I like the wanton cruelty
Of the chimeras one chains up:
Miss Ellen do, pray, pour the tea
Into this charming Chinese cup.

There beneath an angry sky,
A lady, underhand and deep,
Her blue eyes narrow on the cup,
Reveals a naïve ecstasy.
Miss Ellen do, pray, pour the tea.

Théodore de Banville (1823–1891)

THE LOST WINE

One day into the sea I cast
(But where I cannot now divine)
As offering to oblivion,
My small store of precious wine . . .

What, oh rare liquor, willed your loss?
Some oracle half understood?
Some hidden impulse of the heart
That made the poured wine seem like blood?

From this infusion of smoky rose
The sea regained its purity,
Its usual transparency . . .

Lost was the wine, and drunk the waves!
I saw high in the briny air
Forms unfathomed leaping there.

Paul Valéry (1871–1945)

AHOY!

I throw out the kedge anchor
Way far, beyond my reach,
Warping the boat after
—Hour by hour—till a stretch

Of mangrove root frames night.
I throw out the kedge next
Morning—splash—the creek bottom
Gravels; no way on; then elect

To stick in this swamp, this mush
Of wordage till Monday, forever . . . But
At midday hurl out the kedge—
It grips!—we pull forward, a groove

In my mind is no longer battened
Down; I bounce a sponge which comes
Back scrimshaw: color lilts, as
Words do, at harbor, at home . . .

Till, lined as a whale's tooth,
The boat readies; I stretch
To throw out the kedge anchor
Way far, beyond my reach.

JIM I

Sat there
In a folding chair
Awaiting his father:

Sixteen
Is young, if it means
Only more beatings,

Or older
When the boy was ordered
Monthlong to his room last year—

That June crept
By in exploding slow motion; he erupted
July 1st, like a puppy

Ran each four corners
Of the yard, while his mother's
Eyes were gray with tears . . .

Then last week his father loomed
In the doorway:—so framed,
He was shot four times;

Sound
Catapulted against the background
Hill, the slag-dark ground,

To ricochet
From that squat tannery
Which was the future . . .

This much older
Boy, is he in second child-
Hood now? Can he recall

More than that he sat there
In a folding chair
Waiting for his father?

JIM II

Sat there
In a kitchen chair
Eating his dinner:

Twenty-seven
Is young; but then
What next? Often

He'd scoured
Southern back alleys for
Black kids to batter—

No pity
Bled his heart;
Once home, the slag-dark corner

Of his world
Was there: his murdered
Father wielded

Tides like a black
Moon, outstretched
A long marine arm, which

Caught . . . Jim fell.
His sixty-year-old
Heart's failure is real.

ECHO AT MORNING

Great Dane
    As ballerina, aslant
The air; mist
    Is gauze
    On their leaping bodies.

She is
    Joy distilled,
Dancing there, Atalanta,
    A huntress. Oh,
    The moment before

What impends,
    Echo, you spring—
A dog rocking to morning—
    Diana—pure
    Harlequin.

A LITTLE BLUE BOOK

(1912)

Tells of Miss Josie's parlor where
    Breasts of chandeliers
Droop to win all hearts;
    Or in topsy-turvy gala,
Lamps nod over Miss Hilma's costly
    Den—wave like old-timers.

    Our true Sporting District runs
From Thunder way to Storyville,
    Then straight up past the Tenderloin,
Ending over by Bank . . . Miss Grey's
    Palace has ten new Octaroons,
Ladies who'll "please your meanest mood" . . .

Cupids glare down from mirrors, under lights
    At coveralls of skin, pumice,
Shadow—soft as glue or bourbon. All
    Seven orifices lie open now
Like a seal's ear at landfall . . .
    It is the same story, told by gong:

    Man will tunnel woman, spit, groan—
Replace his bowler and his pants—
    He paid. She pays. Creature
Comfort; a moment. Her cage
    Tunnels to etch lines on her face . . .
Miss Birt's door clangs upon red-light day.

TRIANGLE TREE

Tobago, 1980

From its solid base chunk,
    Our Flamboyant tree
    Hurls up proudly
Three branching thigh trunks

Of cinnamon elephant hide,
    Blotched or knighted by pale-green
    Fungus-coins, strewn
On their haunch of copper wood;

We turn to where branches
    Cantilever their long pods,
    Black bananas, ironed,
Staunch,

Twigs verdant as tree toads,
    Or as that iguana, posing
    On clever bent legs, the resin-
Eyed tourist can't goad

Into showing his hideaway-
    In-full-view. This mammoth tree
    And its lizard cousin are surely
There to bless,—just and maximum as day.

WONDERS

We are born and placed among wonders and
surrounded by them, so that to whatever object the
eye first turns, the same is wonderful and full of
wonders, if only we will examine it for a while.

—John de Dondis

Architecture
Describes them in air,
    It builds
Till the highest domes us . . .

At first,
Wonder may blur the eye,
Doubt whittle away, until
Lost in distance, we skid
    To a crisis of confidence,
    As night flies over whistling . . .

Wonders:
    Wind-herded blue
Fields; a stone poem—
Now cut-diamond, wild, true;
A catamaran: dragonfly
In flight over churning
Water; a farmhouse
Breathing through mountain
Windows; the shape of love.

We study, we flick aside
    So many frames, portholes,
    Ways of seeing,—then—
"If only we will examine it"—
One further window
Opens

On this now known
Territory,
Landscape,
Place,
Kin . . .

    Yes.

QUILT OF AN OLD PATTERN

As traveling homeward over our autumn pike,
Cold blooms in these hollows like fog,
Like night: not there, then there all of a sudden—
I, anxious for light, the warm fortress of home,
Knife through a patchwork evening, over the road's
Dark shell, through woods hiding out
Where gray planes fuse to black.

As tenderness, in its gravity, pulls me on
Toward our own terrain, where it may be renewed,
So also on the checkerboard of our lives
There are black squares and red, solitudes
Which cannot be blended; which must not be invaded—
However much, on the plain of our life together,
Like colors on a bolt of Madras
Cloth, longing may lead
Us on, overwhelm, flood us, and we bleed, bleed . . .

LOOKING AT GRANDMOTHER'S

                Grandfather
Clock, I am directed firmly
    To our past, as it clicks on,
        Knitting a parable, a patient outline
        Of days slowly spent . . .

               Husband
Early dead, dressed old before her time
    In long black, a munch of whalebone
        Stays round a thin neck,
        We saw her as living

               Minimally;
—but one day alternating
    Shoes right for left, left-right
        "It rests your feet,"
        Convulsed with laughter . . .

               Then caught
In a revolving door, she went merry-go-
    Round, could not escape . . . Often thought
        Her house afire, wailed from her
        Bedroom window . . .

               Later,
I heard that, older, Grammy went down
    To our plot at nightfall, took off
        Her clothes and, humming, danced
        On an April garden.